Mineral Wells: A Climber's Guide
The Closest Outdoor Climbing Destination in North Texas
By Robert Page

Photography by Robert Page unless otherwise credited

Cover photo: Jacob Dong on *Rachael's Way* (5.10), (page 46)
Photo by: Linux Tung

ISBN: 979-8-35094-336-8

Published and printed in the USA

Contact: MineralWellsClimbing@gmail.com

T0285901

Acknowledgments

To my wife Heather, for your support of my goal to write this book, your patience as I wrote it, your proofreading skills, your invaluable eye for color and design, and most importantly, your love. I love that even though you wouldn't call yourself a climber, you are quick to hop on the wall and give it a try. I love your sense of adventure, your tenacity in life, and your resolve to put up with my climbing addiction.

To Mark Fulmer, who is always ready to take on another adventure at a moment's notice. Mark, your guidance, proofreading, book enhancements, contributions, climbing skills, mentorship, friendship, and spiritual encouragement are all so appreciated. Thank you.

To Blaine Chamberlain, my rock gym and original outdoor climbing partner, it's great to find someone who has the same life-stage difficulties to navigate. I will always remember our late-night conversations in front of the closed Canyons rock gym after a good climbing session, talking about finances, politics, camping, F-150 tow capacity, or "kids today". Thanks, and Gig 'Em.

To Scott, Rafal, Alex, and Jeff, thanks for keeping me going, pushing me to climb harder, and teaching me that you haven't really climbed it until you've down-climbed it.

Why am I writing a guidebook?

It may seem like a silly thing to ask, but I have found myself asking that exact question. Why me? There are tons of people with more skills than me, better climbers than me, who've climbed more routes than me. I'm not a guide. I'm not a dirtbag. I'm not a crusher.

But I am a climber. And a teacher.

Years ago, I remember my search to find the Mineral Wells guidebook that didn't exist. So I did what most have done - what you've probably done - I went online. Luckily everything you read online is trustworthy!
Armed with a basic knowledge and an equally basic set of gear, I ventured to the nearest outdoor location to my DFW home - Lake Mineral Wells State Park's Penitentiary Hollow. I'd be lying if I said it went well. Most of my time was spent wandering around, looking for a climb that looked like it was in my range. The remaining time was spent trying to set up my anchor.
But I have a climbing mantra: *a bad day climbing still beats a good day at work.*
And the more I went, the more fun I had, and the more routes I discovered.

As climbing continued to increase in popularity, as it continues today, I saw more and more climbers want to get outside for the first time. I saw groups arrive at Mineral Wells with a rope and a couple of quick draws, hoping to have a good day on the wall, only to quite literally turn around and go home after realizing they were unable to construct an anchor. Those who stayed constructed less-than-safe climbing setups.
So I began the daunting task of creating this guidebook. Unfortunately, in doing so, it's inevitable that I've mislabeled a route. I'm sure I've offended a First Ascentionist. I've sandbagged ratings. I even named a few routes that aren't on any maps and aren't listed online. You can't please everybody.

My goal in writing this guidebook is to help more climbers to get outside and get more out of their climbing trip than they otherwise would - and do it safely. This book is for you.

Contents

Introduction

How to use this book

Maps

Mineral Wells climbing is categorized by area maps. The table of contents lists each area map or sub-map of each route.

Difficulty

Routes will be designated with one of four colors:

⬤ Cyan = Top-rope routes 5.10 or harder

⬤ Magenta = Boulder routes

◯ Yellow = Top-rope routes 5.9 or easier

Ⓡ Black = Ideal rappel location (requires anchor construction)

Ⓡ↓ Black w/ arrow = Designated rappel location (rap rings available)

Ⓣ Tree

Route Descriptions

All routes are top-rope only, unless otherwise noted. Anchor access from above is noted at the beginning of each area. No First Ascentionist attributions are given for top-rope routes. All routes are between 30-40 ft.

Example:

(Route number)   (Route name)   (Difficulty)   (Route description)

28. Easy Tower (5.7)
Take the center route straight up the tower.

Note that some routes have a difficulty rating in red. This rating reflects the author's revised rating which happens to be different than the Park's rating. Since these routes were originally put up, the ratings system has evolved, holds have broken off, or maybe the First Ascentionist (FA) just sandbagged it. While utmost respect is given to FAs and the work they do to put up routes, this guidebook is for the climber who wants to get outside, perhaps for the first time. A 5.10 gym climber who can't seem to find her way up a sandbagged 5.7 route may become discouraged and give up on outdoor climbing altogether. An outdoor crusher may skip a 5.6 route that climbs like a 5.9, missing out on a great route.

QR Codes

Everyone has a phone. It's time we put them to good use! While not every crag has cell service (this one does!), pictures don't always do it justice. Sometimes tying a knot makes more sense when you **see** it done. That's why this guidebook offers QR Codes - hyperlinks to quick, informative videos. Just scan the QR Code with your phone's camera, and the video link will pop up. HINT: Watch these before you leave home. Don't rely on a cell signal at the crag.

The serenity of Lake Mineral Wells reminds visitors that putting away their electronic devices is good for the soul.

Lake Mineral Wells State Park, home to the Penitentiary Hollow climbing area, has a unique history rooted in superstition and legend. In 1890, James Lynch dug a water well on his land. His wife, who suffered from Rheumatism, drank the mineral-rich water from the well, and her Rheumatism seemed to disappear. Thus began the supposed discovery of the fountain of youth - a cure-all for any ailment. This started a worldwide fascination with what would be called Mineral Wells, Texas. The historic Baker Hotel, built to accommodate the booming town, still stands today as a reminder of how much stock people put in the mineral water's healing properties.[1] (You won't miss it as you drive in to town - it towers over everything else around it!) As the town grew, it quickly exhausted its main water supply and created a new water reservoir - Lake Mineral Wells. The city used the lake for water from 1921 to 1963 when it adopted an alternate source of water. Consequently, in 1975, the city donated the land and lake to the Texas Department of Parks and Wildlife. Six years after it was donated, the State Park was opened.[2]

Penitentiary Hollow, a small sandstone conglomerate canyon, sits just on the end of the lake. The origin of Penitentiary Hollow's name is unclear. According to one opinion, cattle thieves were known to keep their stolen herd in the canyon, using it as a holding area until they moved them on to be sold.

J. A. LYNCH, FOUNDER OF MINERAL WELLS

James Alvis Lynch, Founder of Mineral Wells, photograph, 1907?[7]

Anyone found in the canyon with cattle would be said to have found their way straight to the Penitentiary.[3] Another origin story starts in 1860 and involves two escaped convicts who hid in the area. At the time, there was no lake, and access to the area was quite difficult. There were so many places for the fugitives to hide that the authorities decided to wait it out

Above: A woman and her son pose for a picture in Penitentiary Hollow, circa 1920.[8]

until the fugitives left the hollows in search of food. However, the two convicts refused to leave, and eventually starved to death. From this time forward the area was known as Penitentiary Hollow.[4]

From time to time the infamous Texas bank and train robber, Sam Bass, also used this area as one of his hideouts.[5]

After Lake Mineral Wells was created in 1921, the US Military realized a new use for Penitentiary Hollow: aquatic assault. In 1944-45, in the midst of the second World War, the US Military training center at nearby Camp Wolters aimed to prepare soldiers for battle against the Japanese on foreign soil. Penitentiary Hollow, then a dense, jungle-like terrain with steep rock formations, countless hiding places, and a waterfront, was a perfect training ground for an invasion of Japan, birthing the "Rifle Squad of Offensive Combat", an intense buddy training system of "advance and protection." Troops would arrive by pontoon boat, clear the beach, navigate the rocky terrain, and locate the enemy. Japanese-style huts were erected to add a sense of realism. A team would take about 2 hours to clear the area which at that time was overgrown and rugged. The course culminated with the soldiers scaling the rock structure and engaging the enemy with weapons and hand-to-hand combat.[6] One wonders which modern day routes they took to scale the walls - perhaps *Big Off-width* or *Trash Crack*; perhaps chimneying up The Refrigerator area.

Above: Troops take Penitentiary Cove, at the beach of Penitentiary Hollow, before beginning their training exercise.[9]

Rocks and cliffs rising 60 feet must be scaled . . . above is a picture of one cliff that provides a real test of endurance and skill in ferreting out the Jap . . . everywhere are caves and crevices that may hide an enemy with the fatal bullet . . . The "buddy" system of offensive movement is the key to success in such tactical operations . . . as on one American advances the enemy, his buddy protects him with covering fire . . . Left, a typical bunker is cleaned out—first by grenades, then by rifle fire and cold steel if necessary . . . this takes cool heads . . . Right, two Japs are well on their way to their ancestral homes . . . this American soldier must make sure . . . even the Jap "dead" are tricky, conceal lethal weapons that destroy the unwary soldier who may approach . . . actions in the problem were scrutinized carefully by veterans of south sea campaigns. (Signal Corps Photo.)

Left: Upper photo shows the cliffs of Penitentiary Hollow, with a trainee on the lower right of the photo, and unknown figure (probably either supervisor or simulated "enemy" fighter) upper left.

Lower photo shows a trainee on the beach at Penitentiary Cove. Semi-tropical huts, like the one shown here, were constructed to add to the realism of the exercise.[10]

Even though trips from DFW to Mineral Wells can easily be day trips, overnight camping in the park is a popular option. Lake Mineral Wells State Park has some beautiful camping areas. These areas are very popular and fill up fast. Make sure to take advantage of the park's online reservation system. Weekends are extremely busy and are usually completely sold out months in advance, with the exception of the hot summer months.

The park offers water-only sites, water & electric sites, primitive hike-in tent camping, and equestrian sites. Screen shelters are also available. While no sites currently have RV sewer connections, the park does offer a dump station.
The park maintains hiking, biking, and horse trails. Make sure to pick up a map at the ranger station or look it up online.

Above: A beautiful sunrise over Lake Mineral Wells

Above: An armadillo roots for food in a recently vacated campsite.

Above Left: A curious deer walks through a camper's site.
Above Right: Robert Page and Maddie enjoy a cool morning at a lakeside campsite at Lake Mineral Wells State Park.

Weather is a significant factor in Texas climbing trips. The summer months (June-September) are unbearable at times, with temps commonly reaching over 100 degrees. The lack of breeze in the canyon adds to the stifling humidity, and heat-related illness is a real concern (see "Burned Into My Memory" on page 25). Once cooler weather arrives, it's often accompanied by rain. Due to the fragile nature of wet sandstone, the Park Rangers do a daily assessment, and they will close climbing for the day in wet conditions. You don't want to get there and see this sign! Call ahead to the ranger station's recorded telephone line, updated daily around 8am. As of publishing, the park headquarters phone number is

(940) 328-1171, prompt 1, for area conditions.

Climbing is nearly year-round, with the popular climbing months ranging from September to May.

Penitentiary Hollow is at the south end of the lake. Check in at the headquarters, pay the daily entrance park fee and the small climbing fee. Alternatively, you can purchase an annual Park Pass online or at the Park Headquarters, which pays for everything but the climbing fee. Pick up a map of the park at the Park Headquarters. From there, keep right, and follow the paved road for about 3/4 mile until you come to the parking area for Penitentiary Hollow. Bathrooms, picnic tables, and vending machines are located in this area. From the parking lot, walk North, under the large sign for Penitentiary Hollow. Follow a short trail past the scenic overlook until the path turns left, down a set of natural rock stairs, descending into the canyon. Car to cliff is less than 3 minutes.

Above: The top of the Scenic Overlook, directly above Penitentiary Hollow. You'll see several bolts at the edge of the overlook, but don't forget to take in the view of Lake Mineral Wells.

Above: This gate marks the entrance to Penitentiary Hollow and the short approach trail.

Anchor Building

Itching to get outside on real rock, many new climbers look to Mineral Wells State Park as their first outdoor experience - and for good reason! The wide variety of moderate climbs, short drive from DFW, quick approach, and availability of top-roped routes draw many novices to the park. However, when it comes to building solid top-rope anchors, first-timers to the area are often faced with a disappointing reality.

Anchor building at Penitentiary Hollow is quite unique. Anchor bolts are not at all close to the canyon edge. In fact, most are completely out of reach of the climber. Due to the sandstone quality, the bolts were set back quite a bit - in some cases 10-15 feet back from the canyon edge. This requires climbers to possess a more unique set of anchor-building skills.

The 10+ ft setback on the bolts means you'll need to bring 30-40 feet of material with you.

Here's a list of the recommended anchor-building gear you'll want to have.

- 4 Locking Carabiners
- Bomber anchors will use 1 (or more) of the following:
  - 30+ ft static rope (*recommended*)
  - 30+ ft of cordelette
  - 30+ ft of 1" tubular webbing

The Masterpoint should be *over* the lip of the wall (see figure 1), so the rope does not rub (figure 2) on the rock (bad for the rope, and the sandstone!)

The bolts at Mineral Wells are set back quite a bit from the cliff ledge. Bring plenty of anchor material!

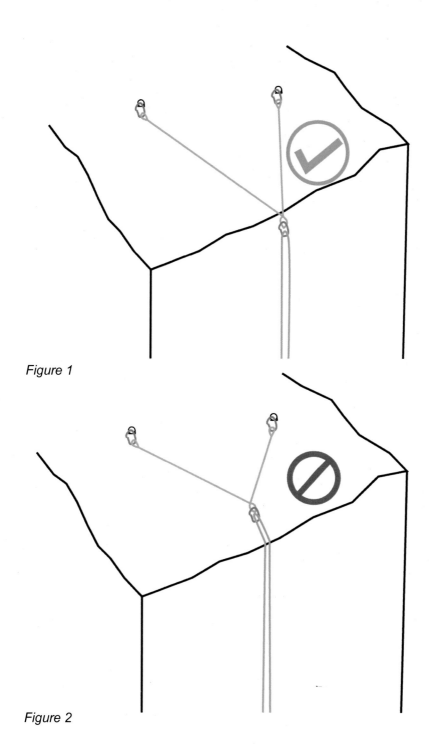

Figure 1

Figure 2

15

Building a SERENE Anchor

Building a safe anchor is a zero-failure activity - meaning there is no room for error without catastrophic, even fatal consequences. Following the acronym SERENE is a helpful way to double-check if your anchor is worthy of trusting your life to.

S - STRONG

Is your anchor strong?
Are the bolts in good condition?
Are your anchor-building materials old or questionable?
Are they rated for climbing?
If using a natural feature like a tree or boulder, is the tree alive, sturdy, and at least 6" diameter?
Can you nudge the boulder with your body weight, even barely?

E - EQUALIZED

Are the legs of your anchor equalized?
Are they sharing equal parts of the load (i.e. the climber) when weighted?

R - REDUNDANT

If any part of your anchor were to fail, is it redundant?
If a bolt were to fail, do you have a backup?
If any part of your anchor gets cut, is there a redundant section to preserve the anchor's integrity? This includes legs of your anchor, as well as your masterpoint.
If your rope were to unclip from a masterpoint carabiner, do you have a second, opposite and opposed carabiner to back it up? (Extra credit if they are locking carabiners)

E - EFFICIENT

Is your anchor an efficient use of time and materials?
If you find you have spend 20 minutes constructing your anchor, and it's full of multiple linked pieces of material, you have introduced extra points of failure. You have also created a situation in which it is often impossible for your partner to understand or decipher whether the anchor is safe.

NE - NO EXTENSION

If any part of your anchor were to fail, would your weight shock-load the redundant anchor?
Shock-loading suddenly and violently puts extreme g-forces on your anchor, and creates the potential for top-rope anchor failure.

Anchor Examples

2-leg Anchor

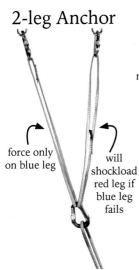

force only on blue leg

will shockload red leg if blue leg fails

- ✓ Strong
- ✗ Equalized
- ✓ Redundant
- ✓ Efficient
- ✗ No Extension

Death-triangle

wide angles multiply forces on bolts

>60°

single strand will fail if cut

- ✗ Strong
- ✓ Equalized
- ✗ Redundant
- ✓ Efficient
- ✓ No Extension

Magic-X

Anchor will shockload if a bolt/ carabiner fails

single strand will fail if cut

- ✓ Strong
- ✓ Equalized
- ✗ Redundant
- ✓ Efficient
- ✗ No Extension

Over-built Anchor

excess gear creates more failure points and difficulty inspecting

- ✓ Strong
- ✓ Equalized
- ✓ Redundant
- ✗ Efficient
- ✓ No Extension

BHK Anchor

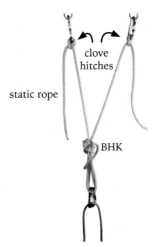

clove hitches

static rope

BHK

- ✓ Strong
- ✓ Equalized
- ✓ Redundant
- ✓ Efficient
- ✓ No Extension

Building a safe anchor at Mineral Wells requires proficiency in several different knot types. The more tools you have in your toolbox, the more places you will be able to safely climb. *Remember: This guidebook is not a substitute for qualified instruction. If you don't have the proper material or knowledge to construct a safe anchor, skip that climb!*

The following knots and hitches are supremely helpful in constructing bomber anchors at Mineral Wells:

BHK (Big Honkin' Knot)

Use: The BHK creates a safe anchor with a minimal length of material while retaining redundancy. It is usually created with static rope, but can be constructed from webbing or appropriate cordelette.

Start by taking a bight of rope, and create another bight *(Fig B1)*:

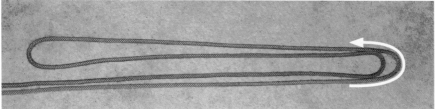

Fig B1

Fold the second bight up *(Fig B2)*, and tie an overhand *(Fig B3)*:

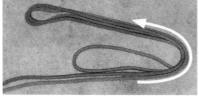

Fig B2

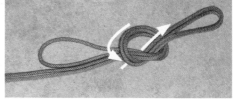

Fig B3

Leaving the tail loop loose can lead to the knot pulling out under tension *(Fig B3)*. Bring the loose tail loop down and clip all three loops *(Fig B4)* with two locking carabiners. Alternatively, loop the tail over the entire masterpoint to prevent it pulling back out once it has been weighted (not shown, see video).

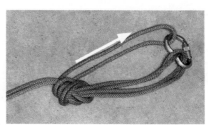

Fig B4

This will keep the tail from potentially slipping out and causing a catastrophic anchor failure.

Scan for video

The Figure Eight on a Bight

Use: This knot is often used to connect a section of a rope to a carabiner.

Bring a bight of rope over itself *(Fig F1)*, then around the back *(Fig F2)*.

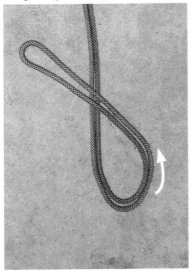

Fig F1

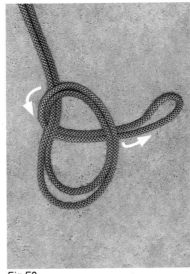

Fig F2

Put the bight through the loop *(Fig F3)* and tighten/dress the knot *(Fig F4)*.

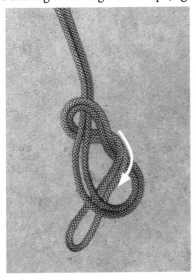

Fig F3

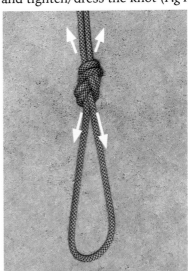

Fig F4

Scan for video

The Clove Hitch

Use: This knot (or "hitch") is used to secure the middle of the rope to something (most often a carabiner). It is used because it's easy to adjust and very easy to loosen once weighted. At Mineral Wells, it's often helpful to fasten at least one leg of your anchor with a Clove Hitch to easily adjust that leg of your anchor.

Create a loop, top strand over bottom. *(Fig C1)*

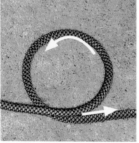

Fig C1

Create a second loop, top strand over bottom. *(Fig C2)*

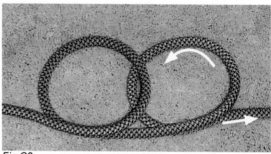

Fig C2

Put the second loop in front of the first loop. *(Fig C3)*

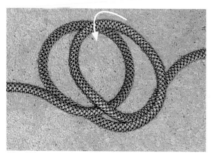

Fig C3

Pass a carabiner through both loops and tighten. *(Fig C4)* The hitch should not move once tight.

Fig C4

Scan for video

The Figure-Eight Tie-In

Use: This knot is the most common type of knot used to tie in to your climbing harness. It's easily recognizable, which makes it easy to check your partner and have your partner check you.

Scan for video

Start by making a figure eight (*Fig E1*). **After** bringing the tail end through two points on your harness, feed the tail through on the left side of the knot (*Fig E2*):

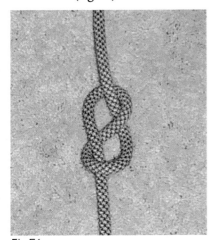

Fig E1

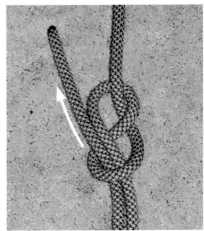

Fig E2

Follow the original strand around (*Fig E3*), passing it back through until it makes a complete figure eight (*Fig E4*). Tighten and dress properly (*Fig E5*).

Fig E3

Fig E4

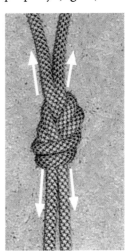

Fig E5

Tethering

A tether is the gear that connects the climber to the masterpoint, both directly (pre-rappel), and indirectly (during the rappel). It is connected with a girth hitch through two points on your harness, and connected to the anchor with a carabiner.

A tether can be the cheapest piece of gear you buy, but it will prove to be one of the most versatile. A tether can keep you from falling from a ledge as you build a top-rope anchor, keep you directly in the anchor as you set up a rappel, and become a rappel extension, creating a more comfortable, potentially safer rappel.

Tethers come in a wide variety, from the Metolius® PAS® (Personal Anchor System) (fig P1), to the Petzl® Connect Adjust® (not pictured), to even a simple sling with an overhand knot tied in it (fig P2).
A tether is a versatile benefit when rappelling, as it allows you to set up your rappel while remaining safe in your anchor (fig P3), and allows you to finally disconnect from the anchor safely on rappel (fig P4).

A tether also extends your rappel device away from loose clothing, long hair, beards, etc, and keeps your Third Hand (see The Third Hand on page 24) backup from jamming in the rappel device.

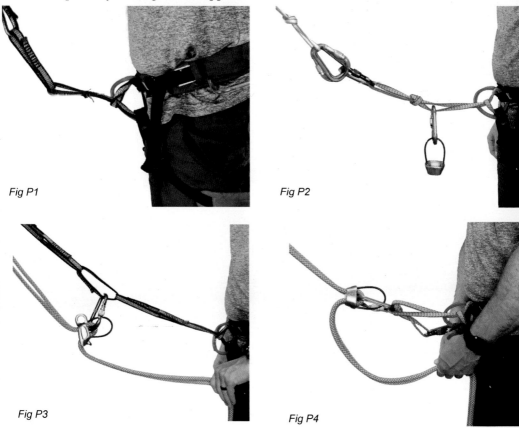

Fig P1

Fig P2

Fig P3

Fig P4

Rappelling is statistically more dangerous than climbing. This is not to deter or discourage you from participating in it, but to highlight the importance of safety.

Begin just as if you are making a top-rope anchor with a redundant masterpoint (fig R1) and two lockers (fig R2). Thread the middle of the rope through both lockers (fig R3) and screw them shut. *Tie a knot in each end of your rope.*

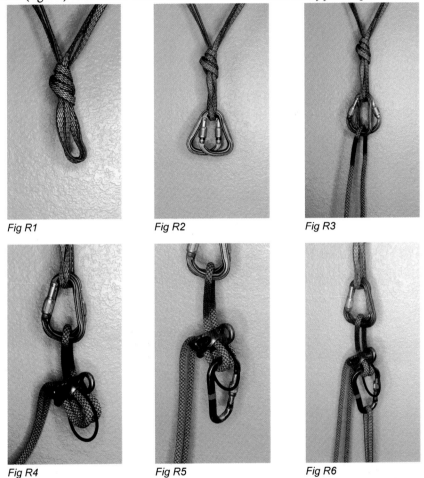

Fig R1   Fig R2   Fig R3

Fig R4   Fig R5   Fig R6

Throw each side of the rope off the ledge to the ground below, *visually confirming the end of each rope is on the ground.* Next add your rappel device by threading a bight of each side of rope through (fig R4).
Capture these two strands with another locker (fig R5). This locker can either be connected to your belay loop directly or attached to a rappel extension (fig R6 - see *Tethering* on page 22). Always weight-test your rappel setup before disconnecting yourself from the anchor!

Scan for video

The Third Hand

A third hand acts as a backup safety device, utilizing friction to "grab" the rope, should you lose your grip on the rappel ropes at any time. This might happen from a rock fall from above, a bee sting, medical condition (i.e. heart attack, heat exhaustion), or simply losing your grip. A third hand is easy to skip, but can prevent an absolutely preventable catastrophe.

Take a third hand or proper cordelette and clip it to your belay loop with a locking carabiner (fig T1). Grab both strands of rope *below* your rappel device. Cross the third hand over both ropes (fig T2). Wrap the ropes at least 3 times (fig T3-T5). *It is essential that the rope and the cordelette be significantly different diameters, or the third hand will not generate enough friction to hold you!*

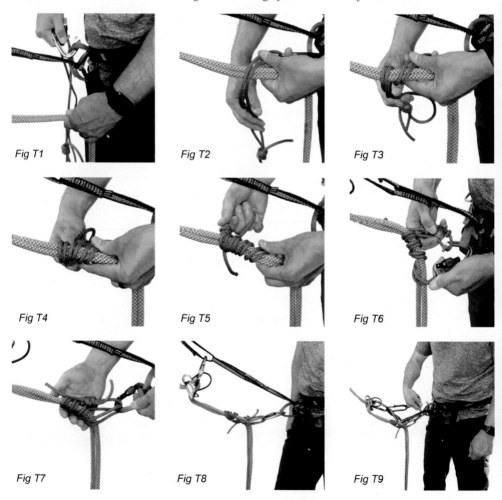

Fig T1

Fig T2

Fig T3

Fig T4

Fig T5

Fig T6

Fig T7

Fig T8

Fig T9

Capture the open end of the third hand with the carabiner (Fig T6) and lock it (Fig T7). Test that it grabs your ropes and supports your weight (Fig T8), then unclip your tether from the masterpoint and attach it to your belay loop (Fig T9) and lock it. *Always test that the rope grabs and holds you before committing your life to it!*

"Burned Into My Memory"

It seemed like a great idea. It was my day off from work in the middle of the week, the kids were out of school, and my wife was game for the adventure. We headed to Mineral Wells for a rare day of outdoor climbing. The gear was loaded into the Suburban, lunches were packed, and off we went. The crags beckoned us onward.

Mineral Wells State Park is a place to climb outdoors. Back in the days before there were half-a-dozen rock gyms in the Dallas Ft. Worth metroplex, Mineral Wells was one of the only places to rock climb at all. It was the perfect place to try outdoor climbing in a close, mellow environment. The base of the climbs in Penitentiary Hollow is downstairs, in the shade, and has an approach measured in minutes.

Back then, on our getaway day, there were no fixed anchors. There were no chains or bolts or even a reliable route map. Your Mineral Wells crag gear included 100 feet of webbing to make top-rope anchors, mostly using the trees which were back from the edge of the routes. So, an ordinary day at Mineral Wells included multiple scrambles up and down the rock to build the anchors, move the anchors, and clean the anchors. Then, do it all again. Of course, that was Dad's job. The scramble to the top was easy. The views at the top of Penitentiary Hollow are glorious, and rapping back to the base is always a kick. The hikers below stop to stare, and they wonder aloud how anyone has the courage to do something as cool and scary and awesome as rock climbing.

The trouble is the top of Penitentiary Hollow is in the sun all day long. On my family's day away, I spent most of the day scrambling up and rapping off, all the while baking unprotected in the relentless Spring sunshine. Then, late in the afternoon, we loaded our filthy selves back into the Suburban. The trouble was, I had unknowingly roasted into a well-done case of acute heat sickness. I wet my pants, nearly vomited, and lay half-conscious in the back of the car while my frightened family wondered if I would die. I wondered too. Come to find out, it was 114 degrees that day. Not kidding. It took much longer to get over feeling completely foolish than the two days it took to recover from my self-inflicted illness.

Rock climbing is the coolest sport. But it's dangerous to practice the coolest sport on the hottest of days. Be careful at Mineral Wells. Take and drink plenty of water. Rest often and rest in the shade. Don't go back to the car, up and down the steps over and over. And be mindful that it's much hotter up top than down in the hollow. Read a little bit about acute heat sickness and true heat stroke. They're not the same thing but both are dangerous. Overheating is a lousy way to get hurt on an otherwise great day of climbing.

CLIMB ON!

- J. Mark Fulmer, MD -

Best Climbs for New Climbers

5. Ledge-End (5.6) - The Refrigerator Area
Good beginner or warm route. Use plentiful jugs and ledges to climb the right side of the slot canyon.

8. Big Off-width (5.6) - Scenic Overview Area
Short climb with lots of holds. A good beginner route, but shorter climbers and kids may find some moves difficult.

40. Sandstone Roof (5.8) - Backside of Main Canyon
A fun jugfest. A couple variations are possible on this hidden gem. Great ledges make this a fun route from start to end. It's possible to top this one out safely.

45. Easy Face #48 (5.6) - Backside of Main Canyon
One of two routes named Easy Face, originally #48 in the park route list. Take the easiest line you see on this wall, up a ramp to a flake, and cruise to the top.

51. Easy Nose (5.6 Sport) - Cave Tower
One of the easiest routes in the park and an excellent route for beginners, new leaders, or kids. Follow the very low angle face, just to the right of the small tree.
(4 bolts, chain with rap rings)

58. Easy Corner (5.5) - Cave Tower
Around the corner from Pee Wee's, scramble up the dihedral for a great lake view.

68. Easy Crack (5.6) - Middle Tower
Follow the obvious crack up giant ledges and plentiful features. Great route for kids and beginners.

71. Unnamed Sport Climb (5.5) - Middle Tower
One of two sport climbs at the park and by far the easiest. A great route for beginners, each bolt is at a solid ledge stance. The top is equipped with two-bolts and donated gear to assist in a rappel or lower.

77. Kiddie Krack (5.4) - Back Tower
Good for kids, or to access the top. There are no bolts here, but there is a large boulder at the top to create an anchor.

81. Boulder Wall D (5.5) - Back Tower
Follow the seam up the very low angle face, or trend right into the dihedral. Good for kids.

Best Climbs in the Park

14. Alaskan Crack (5.8) - Main Canyon Left
Look for a left-side ramp leading to the obvious hand crack that goes about half way up the wall. The crux is getting off the ground without using the ramp. Layback and use high feet, then trend towards the right and top the route.

26. Two Fingers Tequila (5.10) - Main Canyon Left
A fun route with a power move to a small ledge at the crux. A very dirty route that could definitely use some more traffic. Eases up significantly after the crux.

35. Connect the Pockets (5.10) - Main Canyon Right
Start on the tall, vertical pinch grip, making your way up the wall by finding the pockets left and right of your route. Complete a crux move to a ledge, then finish on easy climbing.

40. Sandstone Roof (5.8) - Backside of Main Canyon
A fun jugfest. A couple variations are possible on this hidden gem. Great ledges make this a fun route from start to end. It's possible to top this one out safely.

49. Roof Variation (5.9) - Cave Tower
Start on the slab just to the left of the cave. Pull the fun roof by trending to the right.

54. Gator Head Wall C (5.6) - Cave Tower
Start on the right and use the large horizontal crack to traverse left until the crack dies out, then go up on the easiest section of Gator Head Wall. Fun route!

57. Pee Wee's (5.10) - Cave Tower
One of the best routes in the park! Start right of *Rachael's Way* and follow the chalk up and over the bulge/small roof, making it a bit harder than *Rachael's Way*. After the bulge, find the ledges as the overhang increases dramatically. Enjoy a lake view once you top out.

65. Between Arete and a Hard Place (5.8) - Middle Tower
A very fun route! Follow the seam through the dished out section, finding pockets and pinches, past the small roof onto a steeper top section, with a few hidden ledges at the top. Extend the chains with a double length sling for an easy anchor.

66. Solo Crack (5.9) - Middle Tower
Begin with a layback crux on this pumpy route until the crack widens. At that point, look for pockets to aid your ascent to the top. Watch for creepy-crawlies in the crack, which stays moist in the cooler months.

82. Roof Routes A & B (5.9) - Back Tower
A fun roof on the point of the Back Tower, littered with pockets, jugs, ledges, and a double roof. Climb either side of the arete on the same anchors.

88. Keith's Way (5.11) - Big Overhang
Start at the crescent flake, make your way up to the pockets, then eventually toping out right.

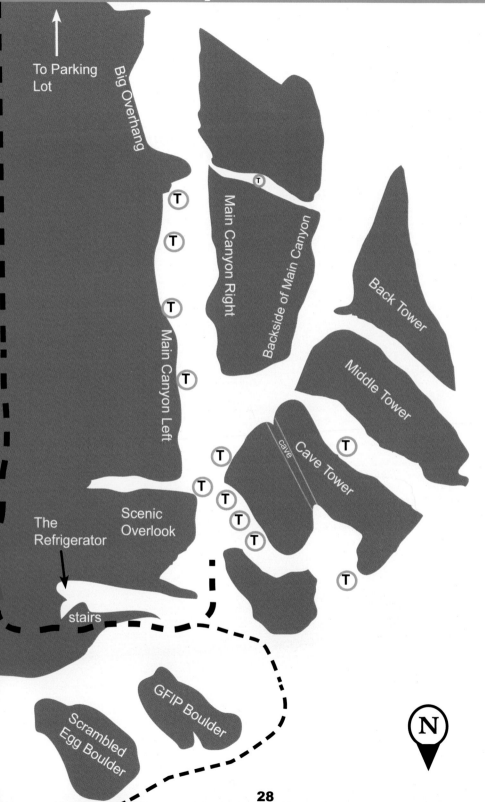

To Parking Lot

Big Overhang

Main Canyon Right

Backside of Main Canyon

Back Tower

Middle Tower

Main Canyon Left

Cave

Cave Tower

Scenic Overlook

The Refrigerator

stairs

GFIP Boulder

Scrambled Egg Boulder

N

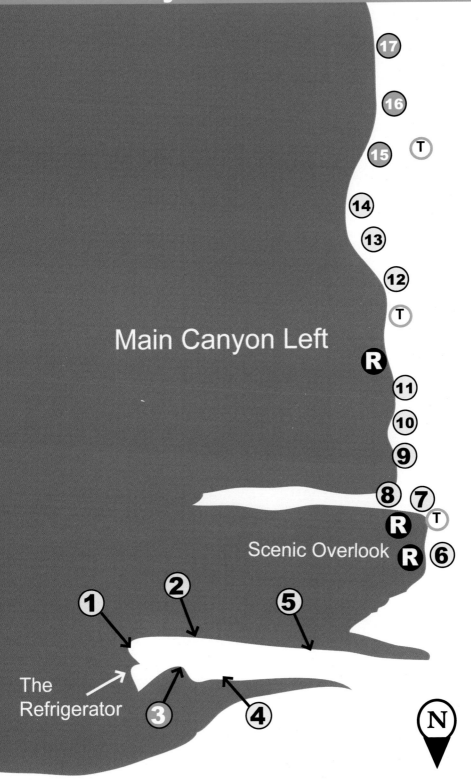

Main Canyon Left

The Refrigerator

Scenic Overlook

Scenic Overlook

The Refrigerator
These routes are often overlooked because of their short height, but can be good warm ups, a relief from the sun (it's cooler in the refrigerator!), or an available route on busy weekends. The stairs actually encircle the Refrigerator and you'll see the canyon (and bolts) before you ever make it down the stairs.

1. A 5.8 Layback (5.8)
Left-layback the off-width crack at the very back of the slot canyon. Top out at the ledge with the bolts, and walk back down the stairs.

2. Arrow Flake (5.8)
Traverse a crack until it meets a small ledge with an arrow-shaped flake above, then climb around the small roof above.

3. Arete (5.10)
Climb the short but challenging arete to the giant ledge above. Spotter definitely needed if not top-roping in the narrow canyon.

4. Dave's Boulder Problem (5.8)
Climb the short wall to the left of *Arete*. There are bolts at the top.

5. Ledge-End (5.6)
Good beginner or warm up route. Use plentiful jugs and ledges to climb the right side of the slot canyon.

Scenic Overlook Area

As the name indicates, this area encompasses the walls on the south and west face of the Scenic Overlook pillar. Anchor bolts are simple to access - just on the other side of the cedar guardrails at the top. While there aren't too many climbs here, you can spend a good amount of time climbing interesting and engaging variations, using the same anchors. *Misc Short Routes* is technically on Main Canyon Left, but is included since it shares anchors with *Big Off-width*.

6. George Hazzard Route (5.8)

West-facing route under the Scenic Overlook. A lot of setup for just one climb. A better rappel route than climbing route.

7. Practice Wall (5.8-5.9)

Route goes right up the middle of the steep, south-facing wall, to the left of *Big Off-width*. In reality, there are probably two or three different routes on this wall that can all be climbed from the same anchor. Balance moves require some technique.

8. Big Off-width (5.6)

Short climb with lots of holds. A good beginner route, but shorter climbers and kids may find some moves difficult.

9. Misc Short Routes (5.7)

Follow the seam to the right of the off-width for easy climbing to the scenic ledge.

Main Canyon Left

This area provides more climbs than any other wall in the park. With climbs ranging from 5.2 to 5.11, there is truly something for everyone here. You'll be hard-pressed to find a weekend when it's not being climbed or rappelled. The crux on most MCL routes will be in the first 8 feet of the climb. The lower sections of the canyon tend to be smoother and steeper than the top sections of the wall. That said - stick with it! Once you get past the opening moves, you're usually in for easier climbing.

The area starts just past the Scenic Overlook, down the long canyon wall South until the canyon narrows to a choke point. This area provides no breeze and can be absolutely stifling in the summer. The wall itself gets shade most of the day, although the climber will have to deal with the blinding sun in the afternoons near the top of each route.

10. A 5.8 Boulder Problem (5.8)

Start at a small ledge directly below a small roof. Traverse right at the roof, then up to the top.

11. Another Dave Problem (5.8)

Start under the hueco, then move left to the seam, following it to the top.

For a variant, move right at the hueco, around the roof, and top out.

12. Short Easy Crack (5.7)
Follow this short, easy crack up the natural line to the top while contemplating how it got its name.

13. Slap Roof (5.8)
Follow the seam between the two cracks, just below the small roof.

14. Alaskan Crack (5.8)
Look for a left side ramp leading to the obvious hand crack that goes about half way up the wall. The crux is getting off the ground without using the ramp. Layback and use high feet, then trend towards the right and top the route.

15. Finger Stinger (5.11)
Find a few small side-pulls and crimps and attack the small seam. Small finger pockets round out the trifecta, leaving you with stinging fingers.

Robert Page on "Alaskan Crack"

33

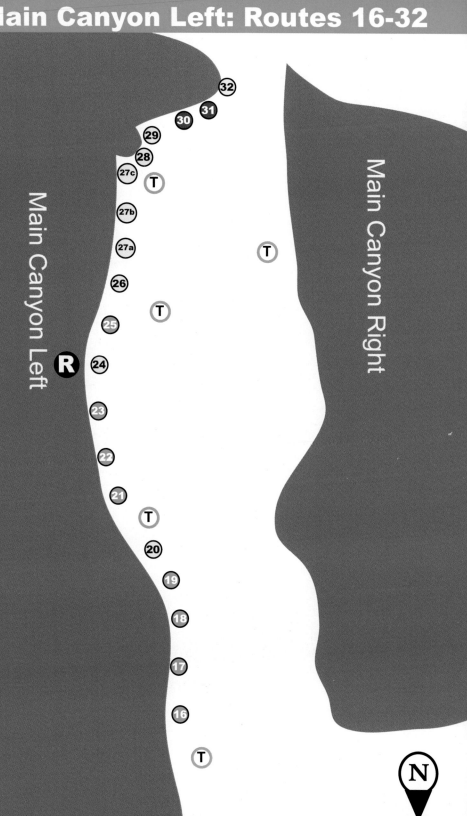

16. Thin Crack (5.10)

Easier climbing than *Finger Stinger*, stay in the seam and look for side-pulls until you get to the flakes about half way up.

17. Bestard (5.10)

Look for small pockets up to an undercling. Good holds are hard to find at the start. Don't give up! Use balance for the first half of the climb, followed by better hands towards the top.

18. A 5.10 Layback (5.10+)

Another moderate, vertical climb. Like *Bestard*, the key is finding your feet. As the route suggests, you'll need to find a few laybacks to make it to the top.

19. Heat Seeker (5.11)

A little bit of everything on the hardest route on MCL. The first half is quite hard. Use small edges up to obvious pocket, then small side crimps to the top. You'll also find side-pulls, gastons, pinches, and more. This route will test your footwork and balance.

20. Hand Crack (5.7)

Follow the obvious crack at the tree. It narrows about half way up, but it still provides enough crimpy holds to get to the top. Despite the easier rating, this is not a particularly kid-friendly route.

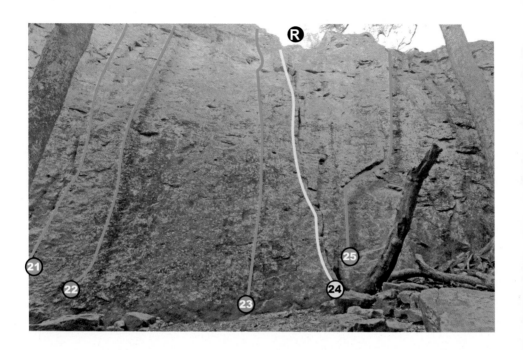

21. Apples to Hell (5.10)
Just to the right of *Hand Crack*, find small flakes and use the crack to find a ledge half-way up. Watch out for moss and lichen.

22. Oz (5.11)
A hard route made harder by lichen. Get to the pocket, then up to a ledge. A slabby climb with thin holds throughout.

23. The Short Unnamed Route (5.10)
Use solid edges to get to the pocket, then easier climbing up top.

24. Another Hand Crack (5.7)
An enjoyable crack climb. The climb tops out on a shelf a few feet from the cliff top, making this an ideal spot to rappel.

25. Something In Between (5.10)
Climb under the large flake, trending right to the pockets. Then use good edges the rest of the way.

26. Two Fingers Tequila (5.10)
A fun climb with a power move to a small ledge at the crux. A very dirty route that could definitely use some more traffic. Eases up significantly after the crux.

27. Moderate to Easy Climbs (5.7-5.9)
A couple variations on an easier, but technical bit of wall. Routes get easier as they go right. Find the single cube of conglomerate for a solid mono edge near the start of 27a. 27c has some fun stemming moves in the obvious dihedral.

28. Easy Tower (5.7)
Take the center-right route up the tower. A bit of route-finding may be necessary.

29. Unfinished Experiment (5.7)
Originally a boulder route, this crack route should be climbed as a rope route, according to park rules and common sense.

30. One Weird (V2)
Use an undercling to start, move up to the obvious pocket, then use side pulls to get to the top.

31. Another Weird (V3)
Pockets, Flakes, Moss, Hard.

32. Downclimb Ramp (5.2)
Use the ramp to downclimb the boulder routes or climb up to access the bolts/parking lot.

The "Gnarly Tree"

Main Canyon Right

Backside of Main Canyon

Main Canyon Right

Halfway along Main Canyon Left, the canyon forks and you're forced either left or right. If you continue left, you stay in the main canyon, and the wall on your right becomes Main Canyon Right (see map). Like much of Main Canyon Left, MCR has more blank walls down low and easier climbing up above. While MCL's slope tends to taper off, MCR is steeper, keeping a near-vertical slope through the entire climb.

Though there aren't as many routes on the wall, there are some really good ones! The top-rope anchor bolts can be reached by accessing the gnarly tree at the south end of the tower where MCL and MCR converge. Scramble and stem up the canyon, using the tree as support. Use ONLY the existing bolts in your anchor setup. Do NOT sling trees per park rules.

Right: The gnarly tree: your access to Main Canyon Right bolts and Backside of Main Canyon bolts

33. Traverse from Mulberry (V2)

34. Rewritten (5.7)
Find edges at the start, then follow the flake, trending right. There are chains with rap rings at the top of this route.

35. Connect the Pockets (5.10)
Start on the tall, vertical pinch grip, making your way up the wall by finding the pockets left and right of your route. Complete a crux move to a ledge, then finish on easy climbing.

36. In Search of Green (5.8)
Climb the seam in the dark section of rock, left of *Connect the Pockets*. This route gets better near the top. Trend right for easier climbing.

37. Green Variation (5.9+)
Trend left and tackle the roof for a harder variation of *ISoG*.

38. Roof Right of Mulberry (5.7)
Start at the small ledge and work your way up through an easy roof with lots of jugs.

39. Line Left of Mulberry (5.7)
Climb the lower angle start on noticeably darker rock than the other routes on this wall.

Left: The "Traverse from Mulberry" extends all the way from "Rewritten" past "Line Left of Mulberry", to the choke point at the south end of MCL and MCR. This area can't be top-roped because of the tree cover interference and thick brush at the top.

Backside of Main Canyon

This area is on the same rock tower formation as Main Canyon Right, but on the opposite side - the side that faces the lake. This wall has some of the harder routes in the park, with the twin 5.11s *Vacation* and *Immigrant* accessible from the same anchor. This area has good tree canopy cover and gets shade most of the day. Access for anchor setup is the same as for Main Canyon Right. Don't "fiddle" with your anchor setup too long, as the top is in full sun, and temps can be 20-30 degrees warmer on top of the rock than down in the shade.

40. Sandstone Roof (5.8)

A fun jug-fest. A couple variations are possible on this hidden gem. Great ledges make this a fun route from start to finish. It's possible to top this one out safely.

41. Right of Immigrant (5.10)

Route starts just left of the crack, past the obvious lower angle rock.

42. Immigrant (5.11)

Start at the obvious ledge and go right into the crux, throwing in a 5.11 move to a crimp, then easier climbing after that.

43. Vacation (5.11-)

Work the beta using the mono pocket to gain a high ledge. Like most routes in the park, the climbing eases up after a low crux.

44. Finger Crack (5.8)
Just to the left of the arete, follow the finger crack up the obvious line. Better holds near the top.

45. Easy Face #48 (5.6)
One of two routes named Easy Face, originally #48 in the park route list. Take the easiest line you see on this wall, up a ramp to a flake, and cruise to the top.

46. Black Flag (5.10+)
Work the boulder beta for the orange rock in the lower half, aiming for a horizontal crack system half way up. Depending on where you climb this, the route may be harder or easier than the grade indicates.

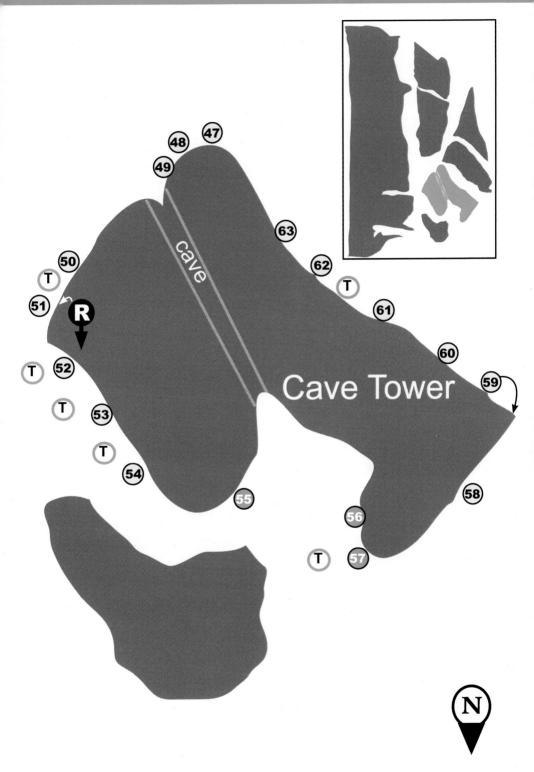

Cave Tower

Cave Tower

Of the three eastern towers, Cave Tower is probably the most popular and sees the most climbing from both beginners and advanced climbers. *Easy Nose* is an excellent beginner lead route (and one of only two lead routes in the canyon), and it's the easiest way to access the top for setting top-rope bolts. *Pee Wee's* is one of the most fun routes in the park, with a roof that provides ledge after ledge of pumpy, exciting climbing.

Access the top-ropes by climbing *Easy Nose*, cheating up *Question Mark*, or stemming up the backside of the cave. *Easy Nose* is recommended.

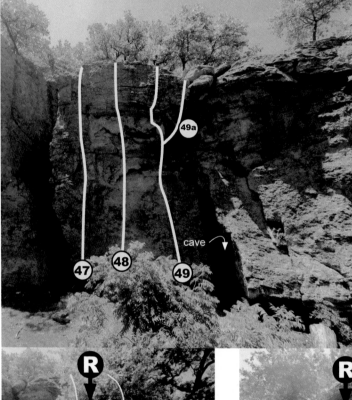

47. Easy Face (5.8)
The left-most climb, to the left of the cave. Stay left to avoid the roof and overhang features, continuing up the face to the diving board feature at the top.

48. Overhang (5.8)
Starting in the middle of the slabby wall, head straight up, keeping the roof on your right and a slight overhang above you.

49. Roof Variation (5.9)
Start on the slab just to the left of the cave. Pull the fun roof by trending to the right.

50. Pocket Buddy (5.7)
Good crimps, low angle, and pockets just where you need them. There are a few lines that can be climbed here. Pick your line and have fun.

51. Easy Nose (5.6 Sport)
One of the easiest routes in the park and an excellent route for beginners, new leaders, or kids. Follow the very low angle face just to the right of the small tree.
Protection: (4 bolts, chains with rap rings)

52. Gator Head Wall A (5.9)
Just around the corner from the bolted *Easy Nose*. Pull on sparse pockets, edges, and crimps, and don't forget your footwork!

53. Gator Head Wall B (5.8)
The middle route on the wall. Navigate the slab until you get to the flake and use the large holds it provides to the top.

54. Gator Head Wall C (5.6)
Start on the right and use the large horizontal crack to traverse left until the crack dies out. Then go up on the easiest section of Gator Head Wall. Fun route!

55. Question Mark (5.10)
The short, but technical climb to the left of the cave (which could be classified as a boulder route). After the first 8-10 feet the route gets much easier in the low 5th class. An alternative method to access the top of the tower is to scramble up the boulder at the base of this climb and hop over onto the "5.easy" section of QM.

The backside of the cave, to the right of *Question Mark*.

56. Rachael's Way (5.10)
Climb the obvious overhanging wall, staying left of the bulge. Then climb up to an ample ledge before merging right to finish at *Pee Wee's*. Pumpy and Fun!

57. Pee Wee's (5.10)
One of the best routes in the park! Start right of *Rachael's Way* and follow the chalk up and over the bulge/small roof. A bit harder than *Rachael's Way*. After the bulge, use excellent ledges to navigate the roof. Enjoy a lake view once you top out.

58. Easy Corner (5.5)
Around the corner from Pee Wee's, scramble up the dihedral for a great lake view.

59. Beastie Boys (5.7)
Start just right of the arete, using pockets and small ledges to an undercling.

60. Easy Routes A (5.7)
Start at the vertical crack and pick your holds up this well-featured area of wall.

47

Cave Tower: Routes 61-63

61. Easy Routes B (5.8)
Start left of the tree, looking for pockets until you get to a ledge near the top. Trend right towards the tree to avoid the vegetation on the ledge here.

62. Easy Routes C (5.7)
Just right of the tree, with good starting feet up to a ledge. Good flakes and low angle finish.

63. Easy Routes D (5.9)
This fun route traverses the horizontal crack until it quits, jogs up, then finishes by topping the route. Take care to set up anchors on the right to avoid swinging on a fall at the crux.

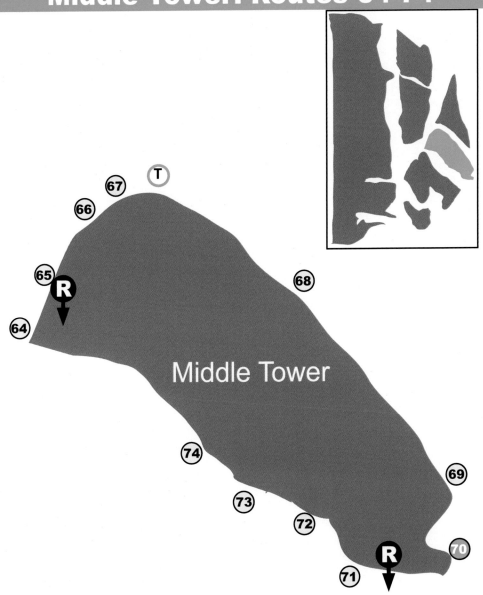

Middle Tower

N

Middle Tower

This tower has some of the better easy-to-moderate routes in the park. This includes the easiest lead climb in the park, *Unnamed Sport Route*, which consists of 3 large ledges and is rated at an easy 5.5. Many first-time leaders have gained experience on this tower. At the time of publication, there are sport bolts at the top, with donated carabiners for an easy rappel. An upgrade to chains and rap rings is unlikely since there are already chains and rap rings at the adjacent corner of this tower near the top of *Arete Solo*. A roof feature on *Sandstone Roof #66* provides good variety on a taller wall, as well as a nice crack climb on *Solo Crack*. Finally, *Dynamo Hum* has two variations of a 5.11 route on the lake side for those looking for more challenging climbing.

Access the top from *Unnamed Sport Route*.

64. Arete Solo (5.6)

Follow the arete by climbing mostly on the north wall, between the towers, for better friction and low angle rock. Remember that you can use the wall behind you. Share the rap anchor bolts for your top-rope.

65. Between Arete and a Hard Place (5.8)

A very fun route! Follow the seam through the dished out section, finding pockets and pinches, past the small roof onto a steeper top section with a few hidden ledges at the top. Extend the chains with a double length sling for an easy anchor.

66. Solo Crack (5.9)
Begin with a layback crux on this pumpy route until the crack widens. At that point, look for pockets to aid your ascent to the top. Watch for creepy-crawlies in the crack which stays moist in the cooler months.

Robert Page climbing *Solo Crack*
photo: Heather Page

67. Gray Streak (5.8)
Left of *Solo Crack* and right of the tree, look for the defined gray water streak running from top to near bottom. Use plentiful pockets and good feet. Use caution topping out, as the tree limbs can get in your way.

68. Easy Crack (5.6)
Follow the obvious crack up giant ledges and plentiful features. Great route for kids and beginners.

69. Sandstone Roof #66 (5.9)
One of two routes with the same name, this one is #66 in the park guide. Follow the giant crack to the roof, then use ledges and make a few exciting moves through the roof.

70a. Dynamo Hum (5.11)
Start in the cave under the roof, working your way up to ledges, then to a vertical headwall with crimps to the top.

70b. Dynamo Hum Variation (5.10)
For an easier variation, start in the large hand crack under the roof, climb up to dual pockets below a large ledge, then an easy top-out.

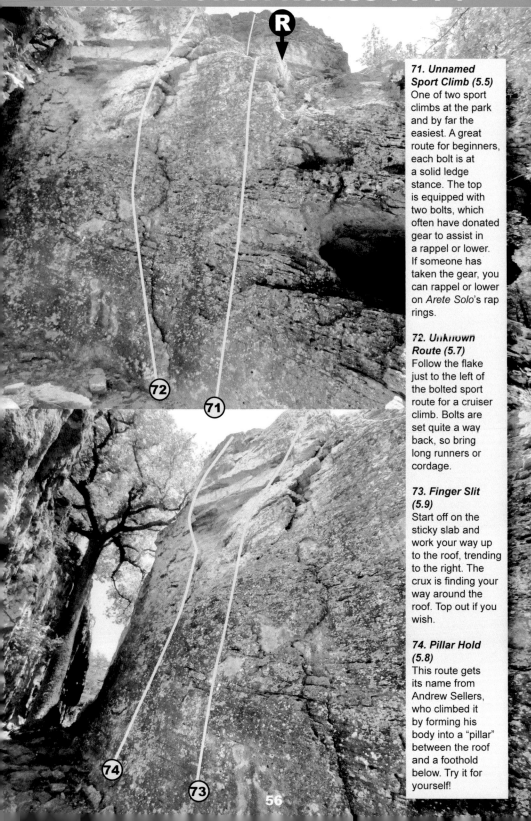

71. Unnamed Sport Climb (5.5)

One of two sport climbs at the park and by far the easiest. A great route for beginners, each bolt is at a solid ledge stance. The top is equipped with two bolts, which often have donated gear to assist in a rappel or lower. If someone has taken the gear, you can rappel or lower on *Arete Solo*'s rap rings.

72. Unknown Route (5.7)

Follow the flake just to the left of the bolted sport route for a cruiser climb. Bolts are set quite a way back, so bring long runners or cordage.

73. Finger Slit (5.9)

Start off on the sticky slab and work your way up to the roof, trending to the right. The crux is finding your way around the roof. Top out if you wish.

74. Pillar Hold (5.8)

This route gets its name from Andrew Sellers, who climbed it by forming his body into a "pillar" between the roof and a foothold below. Try it for yourself!

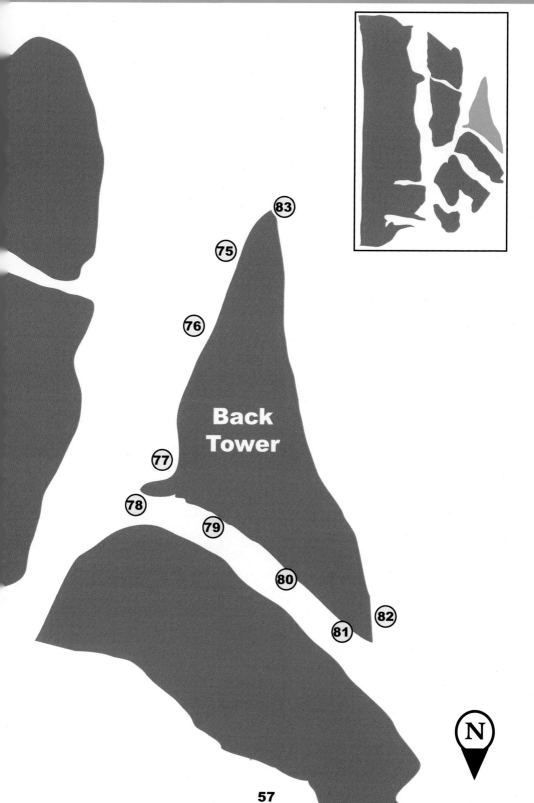

Back Tower

This is the triangular tower formation in the back of the Hollows area. This area probably sees the least amount of traffic due to its low number of established routes and low grade for many of its climbs. Access the top via *Kiddie Krack* or a gully on the backside (lakeside) of the formation.

75. Cattle Crack (5.6)

Follow the seam left of *Pocket Sockets*. Starts below a ledge with two pockets, then over a bulge to gain a ledge and top out to the right, avoiding briars.

76. Pocket Sockets (5.6)

Look for the large pockets resembling eye sockets. Start to the right, then follow the black water streak.

77. Kiddie Krack (5.4)

Good for kids or to access the top. There are no bolts here, but there is a large block at the top to create an anchor.

78. Boulder Wall A (5.7)
Lots of pockets, several ledges, great
texture, and some low angle climbing,
just right of the arete.

79. Boulder Wall B (5.7)
Start in a dished out section over to a very defined, slanted roof. Low angle, but steeper than others on this wall.

80. Boulder Wall C (5.6)
Follow the large flake from bottom to
top. Low angle climbing that's good for
beginners.

81. Boulder Wall D (5.5)
Follow the seam up the very low angle
face, or trend right into the dihedral.
Good for kids.

81

82. Roof Routes A & B (5.9)
A fun roof on the point of the Back Tower, littered with pockets, jugs, ledges, and a double roof. Climb either side of the arete on the same anchors.

82a

82b

83. Break Rock (5.9)
A very bouldery start with multiple pockets, side pulls, and a difficult roof move. Multiple variations exist.

83

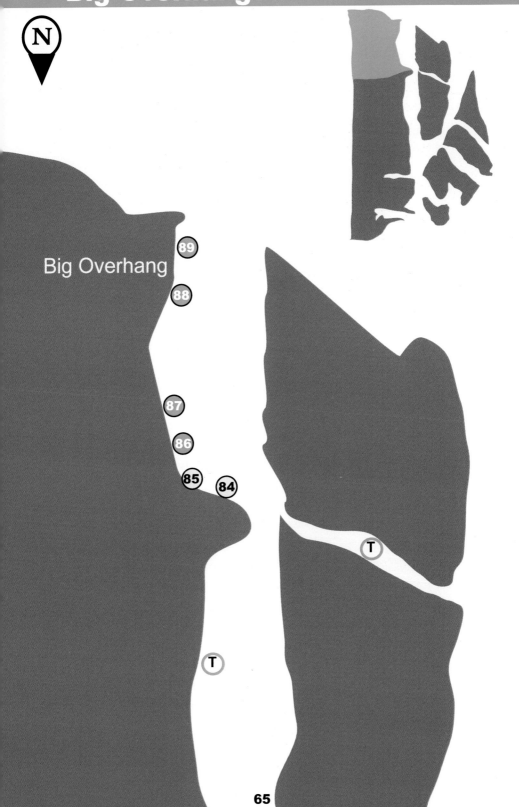

Big Overhang

Big Overhang Area
This area starts just south of the bottleneck where MCL and MCR meet. It has the hardest climb in the park, and the most impressive looking rock on a giant, overhanging, 40 ft wall. In Summer, a poison ivy vine grows in the middle of the wall - take note!
Access the anchors from the approach path before you descend into the canyon.

84. Crumbly (5.9)
A long-lost route originally listed in *Texas Limestone II*. Climb the seam to the left of *Trash Crack* using flakes and shallow pockets. No anchor, unless you use the anchor bolts from *Trash Crack*.

85. Trash Crack (5.5)
Climb the obvious off-width crack. Plentiful holds abound. Either climb on the face, or use the crack. The only easy route in this area.

86. Thieves & A**holes (5.10+)
This route probably got its name from Penitentiary Hollow's reputation for cattle thieves and their booty's booties. Start midway between *Trash Crack* and a large, detached flake near *Hidden Jewel*, making your way up to the crescent ledge. Grab the pocket, then look up for a side pull and a ledge before attacking the overhang. Pumpy, fun climbing!

87. Hidden Jewel (5.11)
Start just to the left of the large flake on the ground, often covered in poison ivy. Climb to the pocket, then up to another, before battling it out with the overhang, trending either right or left for a challenging finish.

88. Keith's Way (5.11)
Start at the crescent flake, traverse a ledge, make your way up to the pockets, then complete the crux moves, and eventually top out right.

89. Gandolf (Won) (5.12)
Start at the low horizontal crack with two obvious handholds and follow the blunt arete. Find a small hidden ledge, ending up at the top of *Keith's Way*. (Originally named *Gandolf*, now referred to as *Gandolf Won* in the park guide)

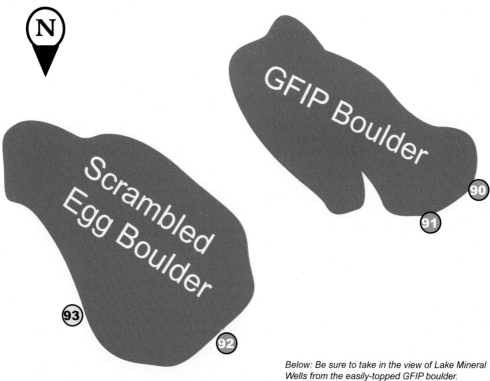

N

GFIP Boulder

Scrambled Egg Boulder

90

91

93

92

Below: Be sure to take in the view of Lake Mineral Wells from the easily-topped GFIP boulder.

GFIP Boulder

As you first enter the Hollows via the stone staircase, take the trail to the right for 50 feet and you'll come upon GFIP. This boulder only has 2 established routes, but they are good ones. There are anchor bolts at the top, set back in typical Mineral Wells fashion. Access the top via the backside scramble. If you feel uneasy about the scramble, you're not in the right spot.

90. Unprepared (5.11)
Climb the middle of the face to a pocket up under the roof. The crux comes getting around the roof to the top.

91. GFIP (5.10+)
A colorful way of saying "I'm Pumped!", this route follows the crack up to a large pocket, then gains a ledge before moving right to the finish.

Scrambled Eggs Boulder
Just past GFIP Boulder, this boulder also has an easy "scramble" up the back to setup an anchor. There are no bolts here. Sling the chickenheads at the top for a bomber anchor, but pay close attention to the direction of pull. You'll likely have to adjust your anchor if climbing both routes.

92. Scrambled Eggs and Chickenheads (5.11/V3)
The crux is getting off the ground on this very high start. Small edges and good flexibility are key to climbing this short route to gain the first ledge. "5.easy" climbing after that. It's more of a bouldering route, and you'll definitely want a spot off the ground.

93. Pop's Memorial (5.7)
Left and around the corner from *Scrambled Eggs & Chickenheads.* Follow the flake up the face.

Route List (by difficulty)

Route List (alphabetically)

A

A 5.8 Boulder Problem
5.8; p32

A 5.8 Layback
5.8; p30

A 5.10 Layback
5.10; p35

Alaskan Crack
5.8; p33

Another Dave Problem
5.8; p32

Another Hand Crack
5.7; p36

Another Weird
V3; p37

Apples to Hell
5.10; p36

Arete
5.10; p30

Arête Solo
5.6; p50

Arrow Flake
5.8; p30

B

Beastie Boys
5.7; p47

Bestard
5.10; p35

Between Arete and a Hard Place
5.8; p50

Big Off-width
5.6; p31

Black Flag
5.10+; p42

Boulder Wall A
5.7; p59

Boulder Wall B
5.7; p60

Boulder Wall C
5.6; p61

Boulder Wall D
5.5; p62

Break Rock
5.9; p64

C

Cattle Crack
5.6; p58

Connect the Pockets
5.10; p39

Crumbly
5.9; p66

D

Dave's Boulder Problem
5.8; p30

Downclimb Ramp
5.2; p37

Dynamo Hum
5.11; p55

Dynamo Hum Variation
5.10; p55

E

Easy Corner
5.5; p47

Easy Crack
5.6; p53

Easy Face
5.8; p44

Easy Face #48
5.6; p42

Easy Nose
5.6; p44

Easy Routes A
5.7; p47

Easy Routes B
5.8; p48

Easy Routes C
5.7; p48

Easy Routes D
5.9; p48

Easy Tower
5.7; p37

F

Finger Crack
5.8; p42

Finger Slit
5.9; p56

Finger Stinger
5.11; p33

G

Gandolf (Won)
5.12; p67

Gator Head Wall A
5.9; p45

Gator Head Wall B
5.8; p45

Gator Head Wall C
5.6; p45

George Hazzard Route
5.8; p31

GFIP
5.10+; p69

Gray Streak
5.8; p52

Green Variation
5.9+; p40

H

Hand Crack
5.7; p35

Heat Seeker
5.11; p35

Hidden Jewel
5.11; p66

I

Immigrant
5.11; p41

In Search of Green
5.8; p40

K

Keith's Way
5.11; p67

Kiddie Krack
5.4; p58

L

Ledge-End
5.6; p30

Line Left of Mulberry
5.7; p40

M

Misc Short Routes
5.7; p31

Moderate to Easy Climbs
5.7-5.9; p37

O

One Weird
V2; p37

Overhang
5.8; p44

My Tick-list

#	Route Name	Date Climbed / Notes
1	A 5.8 Layback	
2	Arrow Flake	
3	Arete	
4	Dave's Boulder Problem	
5	Ledge-End	
6	George Hazzard Route	
7	Practice Wall	
8	Big Off-width	
9	Misc Short Routes	
10	A 5.8 Boulder Problem	
11	Another Dave Problem	
12	Short Easy Crack	
13	Slap Roof	
14	Alaskan Crack	
15	Finger Stinger	
16	Thin Crack	
17	Bestard	
18	A 5.10 Layback	
19	Heat Seeker	
20	Hand Crack	
21	Apples to Hell	
22	Oz	
23	The Short Unnamed Route	
24	Another Hand Crack	
25	Something in Between	
26	Two Fingers Tequila	
27	Moderate to Easy Climbs (a, b, c)	
28	Easy Tower	
29	Unfinished Experiment	
30	One Weird	
31	Another Weird	
32	Downclimb Ramp	
33	Traverse from Mulberry	

#	Route Name	Date Climbed / Notes
34	Rewritten	
35	Connect the Pockets	
36	In Search of Green	
37	Green Variation	
38	Roof Right of Mulberry	
39	Line Left of Mulberry	
40	Sandstone Roof	
41	Right of Immigrant	
42	Immigrant	
43	Vacation	
44	Finger Crack	
45	Easy Face #48	
46	Black Flag	
47	Easy Face	
48	Overhang	
49	Roof Variation	
50	Pocket Buddy	
51	Easy Nose	
52	Gator Head Wall A	
53	Gator Head Wall B	
54	Gator Head Wall C	
55	Question Mark	
56	Rachael's Way	
57	Pee Wee's	
58	Easy Corner	
59	Beastie Boys	
60	Easy Routes A	
61	Easy Routes B	
62	Easy Routes C	
63	Easy Routes D	
64	Arete Solo	
65	Between Arete and a Hard Place	
66	Solo Crack	
67	Gray Streak	

My Tick-list

#	Route Name	Date Climbed / Notes
68	Easy Crack	
69	Sandstone Roof #66	
70	Dynamo Hum/Variation	
71	Unnamed Sport Climb	
72	Unknown Route	
73	Finger Slit	
74	Pillar Hold	
75	Cattle Crack	
76	Pocket Sockets	
77	Kiddie Krack	
78	Boulder Wall A	
79	Boulder Wall B	
80	Boulder Wall C	
81	Boulder Wall D	
82	Roof Routes A&B	
83	Break Rock	
84	Crumbly	
85	Trash Crack	
86	Thieves & A**holes	
87	Hidden Jewel	
88	Keith's Way	
89	Gandolf (Won)	
90	Unprepared	
91	GFIP	
92	Scrambled Eggs & Chickenheads	
93	Pop's Memorial	

Bibliography

[1] https://www.mineralwellstx.com/history/
[2] https://tpwd.texas.gov/state-parks/lake-mineral-wells/park_history
[3] https://texashistory.unt.edu/ark:/67531/metapth25094/
[4] Eddins, Howard B. The Longhorn (Camp Wolters, Tex.), Vol. 4, No. 30, Ed. 1 Friday, January 19, 1945, newspaper, January 19, 1945; Camp Wolters, Texas.
[5] ibid
[6] ibid
[7] James Alvis Lynch, Founder of Mineral Wells, photograph, 1907?; (https://texashistory.unt.edu/ark:/67531/metapth16136/: accessed November 25, 2022), University of North Texas Libraries, The Portal to Texas History, https://texashistory.unt.edu; crediting Boyce Ditto Public Library, Special Collections.
[8] [Penitentiary Hollow], photograph, Date Unknown; (https://texashistory.unt.edu/ark:/67531/metapth25094/: accessed October 17, 2022), University of North Texas Libraries, The Portal to Texas History, https://texashistory.unt.edu; crediting Boyce Ditto Public Library, Special Collections.
[9] Eddins, Howard B. The Longhorn (Camp Wolters, Tex.), Vol. 4, No. 30, Ed. 1 Friday, January 19, 1945, newspaper, January 19, 1945; Camp Wolters, Texas. (https://texashistory.unt.edu/ark:/67531/metapth601208/: accessed October 17, 2022), University of North Texas Libraries, The Portal to Texas History, https://texashistory.unt.edu; crediting Boyce Ditto Public Library, Special Collections.
[10] ibid

Trademarks
Metolius and PAS are registered trademarks of Metolius Mountain Products Inc.
Petzl and Connect Adjust are registered trademarks of Big Bang.

About the Author

photo: Mark Fulmer

Robert Page is a life-long DFW resident currently living in Frisco, TX. He is a husband to Heather, and father to two beautiful girls. Together they have 3 amazing dogs, Joey, Maddie, and Rambo.

When not at his day job, you can find Robert at the rock gym, camping with his family, or planning his next climbing trip.

Robert's background in digital printing, love for teaching, and belief that "a picture is worth a thousand words" led him to create a book that will hopefully help other climbers, and broaden appeal and access for the beloved sport of rock climbing and the great outdoors.

Questions and Comments?
MineralWellsClimbing@gmail.com

photo: Heather Page

The Author on one of many family climbing trips to Lake Mineral Wells State Park
Route: "Pocket Buddy"

photo: Heather Page

Rambo: world's best crag dog and loyal belayer.